The Secret Method to Conscious Love

Workbook Journal

Deepen Understanding of Yourself and
Improve Your Dating & Relationships

ANGELA N. HOLTON

THE SECRET METHOD TO CONSCIOUS LOVE

WORKBOOK JOURNAL

Deepen Understanding of Yourself and Improve Your Dating & Relationships

By Angela N. Holton

Little Kobi Bear, LLC
info@lovesanctuary.com
www.lovesanctuary.com

ISBN-13: 978-0-578-89217-7

Printed in the United States of America.

This book is dedicated to all of my beautiful sisters who still believe in love.
I hear you. I see you.
I am with you.

"My great hope is to laugh as much as I cry; to get my work done and try to love somebody and have the courage to accept the love in return."
~Maya Angelou

CONTENTS

Before beginning, let's set your intention. What is your relationship intention and reasons for completing this workbook? Write your own intention and dedication here:

_____

_____

_____

_____

_____

_____

_____

_____

_____

_____

PROLOGUE

"Your task is not to seek for love, but merely to seek and find all the barriers within yourself that you have built against it."

~Rumi

*I*f this workbook journal has found its way into your hands, chances are you are single and perhaps frustrated, overwhelmed, and confused with the current dating culture. Perhaps you desire to change your dating experiences and attract better and healthier relationships. I completely understand your feelings, for I too have been there.

Women who come to me for support are often struggling around their singleness. They express feelings of loneliness, sadness, desperation, hopelessness, fear, anger and mental anguish. I understand all of those feelings too, because, again, I have been there.

Today's dating narrative is anything but clear and simple. There are no more rules or boundaries. Expectations and standards seem lower than they used to be. Anything goes in the modern dating space, which makes navigating it very challenging. In fact, it seems almost impenetrable. Our culture has become increasingly reliant on technology, and therefore, connecting with someone organically is exponentially harder. As we cannot practice relationships without being in relationships, many of us find ourselves dealing with a catch-22.

But what if we created a new mindset around dating? What if women considered the paradigm from a different perspective, so that dating became less about "finding someone" and more about "becoming the person we seek?" What if we began to see our dating experiences as reflections of ourselves and thus as a platform to grow in self-awareness and self-knowledge?

What if dating was not just about the destination (i.e. the "ideal" relationship) but an exciting path to self-discovery — an opportunity to uncover our fears, self-judgments and self-sabotage, as well as our unconscious beliefs around love and relationships?

In doing so, we might also examine our relationship patterns so that we can break free from old unhealthy cycles and create newer, healthier habits. We may also re-experience old emotions and relationship "ghosts" that still haunt us and learn to exorcise them so they no longer control us.

This is The Conscious Love & Dating Method™ approach.

The Conscious Love & Dating Method™ is about using the modern dating arena to enhance self-awareness, emotional intelligence, self-love, self-knowledge, and to cultivate and practice skills that are needed for healthy partnership.

Gone is any narrative that makes women feel desperate and longing for partnership. Instead, we are empowered by the understanding that we are embarking on our path of self-discovery. There are no "bad dates," just opportunities to peel a layer back and to learn something new about ourselves.

So, too, is the purpose of this journal workbook. Journaling serves as a bridge, helping us connect the conscious from the unconscious. As you date, and write about your dating experiences, your relationship patterns will begin to emerge. You will be able to see more of the old wounds and triggers, the fears and self-sabotaging behaviors that may be keeping successful relationships at bay, and then begin to address the changes and healing that need to take place in order for you to attract and cultivate the healthy relationship you desire. You will also have a clearer vision of your ideal partner.

The journal is comprised of various method exercises designed to help you explore deeper parts of yourself. In one section, you will journal freely in response to questions. At the end of each section, you will then be asked to write something new you've discovered about yourself. Additionally, affirmations, or positive self-talk statements, are included at the end of each section to support your new way of thinking, as well as supplemental space for you to create affirmations of your own.

Lastly, at the back of the book you will find additional space for your freestyle journaling and notes. This space is allocated for you to express your deeper thoughts and reflections that may arise during or after each section.

When we know better, we do better. So while we will write freely and authentically in this journal, we will not judge ourselves. We will offer ourselves compassion, grace, and patience. We will date with greater "consciousness," thus, each date will serve as a mirror, revealing the parts of us that we can heal and transform.

Let the dating journey begin...

"What you seek is seeking you"
~ Rumi

METHOD ONE

Self-Love & Self-Worth

"What is love? Love is treating your beating heart with a great deal of tenderness, with understanding, love, and compassion. If you cannot treat your own heart this way, how can you treat your partner with understanding and love."

~ Thich Nhat Hanh

Before beginning a journey toward a relationship, it's important to check in on how we are feeling about ourselves. Below are some fundamental questions to ask yourself before inviting someone else to share in your life.

Spend a few moments answering the following questions.

1. Do you like who you are and the woman you're becoming?

_____

_____

_____

_____

_____

_____

_____

_____

2. Do you feel generally good about yourself on a day-to-day basis?

_____

_____

_____

_____

_____

_____

_____

_____

3. How do you feel about your life purpose and goals?

_____

_____

_____

_____

_____

_____

_____

_____

_____

4. Are you happy? Are you looking for someone or something to make you happy? Answer honestly. No one else will see this but you.

_____

_____

_____

_____

_____

_____

_____

_____

_____

5. Have you acknowledged and healed from your past hurts?

_____

_____

_____

_____

_____

_____

_____

_____

_____

_____

6. What do you believe you deserve in life? In a relationship?

_____

_____

_____

_____

_____

_____

_____

_____

_____

_____

"When we feed and support our own happiness, we are nourishing our ability to love. That's why to love means to learn the art of nourishing our happiness."
~Thich Nhat Hanh

Creating a healthy and loving relationship requires us to constantly look in the mirror and closely examine who we see. If we don't like ourselves or enjoy our own company, how can we expect anyone else to like us?

Sometimes we struggle to like ourselves and to feel worthy of love, perhaps because our parents were unable to mirror love to us in the way we needed to be loved, or because of other past relationships that disappointed us. As a result, we may choose relationships that re-enact our old story and play out our unconscious belief that "I'm not worthy or good enough for love."

Lacking respect and love for Self can make us prey for emotional predators — partners who take advantage of our old wounds in order to manipulate and control us. Women give their partners constant direction and permission on how to treat us. Thus, if we feel badly about ourselves, we'll give the partner in our life unconscious signals to treat us in the same way. It is therefore imperative that we enter into dating relationships with a healthy sense of self-worth and self-respect.

Additionally, when we feel unhappy, afraid, lonely, and insecure, we may seek partnership to make us feel better about ourselves and about our future. We may make someone else responsible for our "wholeness" and happiness. These are God-sized needs and fulfilling them is an impossible task, even for the best of us. In order to have a healthy relationship we must first understand that we alone are accountable for our lives.

We don't attract what we say we want.
We attract what we feel worthy of.

In this section of the journal, we are laying down the foundation in understanding our self-worth.

The most important thing to remember when starting the dating journey is to know and believe in our hearts that we're already good enough for a relationship. We are the most loved and prized creation and possession of the great Creator and we cannot be separated from our Divine Source.

This means we don't need to be perfect in order to be loved by another. We don't need to lose the weight, have the right job, the right amount of money in our bank accounts, or have solved all of our problems in order to be deserving of love. We are worthy of love now.

Before beginning your dating journey, journal answers to the following questions as openly and honestly as possible.

1. I believe I deserve _____

_____

2. In relationships, I believe I deserve _____

_____

3. My parents showed me love by _____

_____

4. What I learned from my parents about what I deserve is ___

_____

5. I feel worthy of _____

_____

6. I show love to myself by _____

_____

7. During my childhood, I wish I received more _____

_____

"To love without knowing how to love wounds the person we love."
~ Thich Nhat Hanh

8. I feel best about myself when I _____

_____

9. I feel most loved when _____

_____

10. I love myself when _____

_____

11. I struggle to love myself because _____

_____

12. I feel proud of myself because _____

_____

13. I would be ready for a relationship if I _____

_____

14. The things I love about myself are _____

_____

15. In my past relationships I have been _____

_____

When you are finished, reread your entries. What have you learned about yourself?

_____

_____

_____

_____

_____

_____

_____

_____

_____

_____

_____

_____

_____

_____

_____

_____

_____

_____

_____

_____

_____

_____

_____

_____

_____

_____

_____

_____

Affirmations:

I deeply and completely love and approve of myself.

I am loved. I am loving. I am lovable.

I am good enough.

I am good enough just as I am for a loving and committed relationship.

I am deserving of love and to be loved.

Write your own affirmations here:

_____

_____

_____

_____

_____

_____

_____

"You, yourself, as much as anybody in the entire universe, deserve your love and affection."
~Buddha

METHOD TWO

Releasing the Inner Critic

"If you knew how powerful your thoughts are,
you would never think a negative thought."

~Peace Pilgrim

*I*n this section we are going to learn more about that pesky little negative voice that tells us we're not good enough. The one that alternates between a roar and a whisper so soft we barely know it's there, the one that says: *we'll fail, that no one cares, that no one will ever love or choose us.*

All living creatures – plant, animal and human – thrive in a loving and supportive environment. They do not thrive in hostility and negativity. Our thoughts and the words we speak to ourselves have the power to speak life or death to us. Our thoughts directly impact our beliefs about ourselves, which then impacts our mood and emotions. Our emotions then drive our behaviors and actions, therefore, if we want to feel good, grateful, abundant, and ready to attract love, our thoughts need to align with "feel good" thoughts. On the other hand, when we berate and condemn ourselves, our thoughts lead to the belief that we are not good enough and unworthy, which then engenders a negative reflection of oneself and emotions rooted in sadness, depression, loneliness, despair, and hopelessness.

The good news is we have the power to choose the thoughts and opinions we have of ourselves, and which ones we believe to be true. We can control our "monkey mind" – that part of the brain that runs our thoughts and beliefs on a loop.

When we see ourselves going down the rabbit hole of negative self-talk and judgment, we can catch and remind ourselves to choose more loving, compassionate, and helpful thoughts. Loving ourselves means noticing our inner-critic and taking intentional and conscious actions to silence it — focusing on our strengths, embracing our flaws and vulnerabilities, and tapping into our inner cheerleader.

A conscious person has an increased awareness of her thoughts, words, behaviors and actions. A conscious dater is simply some-one who applies this awareness to her romantic life. Under-standing our internal narrative and mastering control over our unconscious and conscious negative self-talk is the first step toward this awareness and toward success in every area of life, including dating.

Journal the following questions to learn more about your positive and negative thoughts.

1. I criticize myself for _____

_____

_____

2. I learned to criticize myself from _____

_____

_____

3. I was criticized mostly by _____

_____

_____

4. They criticized me for _____

_____

_____

5. Five things I like about myself:

a. _____

b. _____

c. _____

d. _____

e. _____

6. Five things I don't like about myself:

a._____

b._____

c._____

d._____

e._____

7. Which things can I change about myself?

_____

_____

_____

_____

_____

"Keep your thoughts positive because your thoughts become your words. Keep your words positive because your words become your behavior. Keep your behavior positive because your behavior becomes your habits. Keep your habits positive because your habits become your values. Keep your values positive because your values become your destiny."

~Mahatma Gandhi

8. How can I begin creating a small change today?

_____

_____

_____

9. What I believe most about myself is _____

_____

_____

10. What I mostly say to myself is _____

_____

_____

11. I often say the following positive things to myself _____

_____

_____

12. I often say the following negative things to myself _____

_____

_____

13. I could cheer myself on when I _____

_____

_____

_____

Review your entries. What did you learn about yourself from this section?

_____

_____

_____

_____

_____

_____

_____

_____

_____

_____

_____

_____

_____

_____

_____

_____

_____

_____

_____

_____

_____

_____

_____

_____

What did you learn about yourself from your date?

_____

_____

_____

_____

_____

_____

_____

_____

_____

_____

_____

_____

_____

_____

_____

_____

_____

_____

_____

_____

_____

_____

_____

Affirmations:

I release my inner critic and choose to love and accept myself unconditionally.

I choose loving thoughts.

I choose to see myself in the brightest light.

The thoughts I choose magnify how I feel about myself.

Write your own affirmations here:

_____

_____

_____

_____

_____

_____

_____

"We tend to think being hard on ourselves will make us strong. But it is cherishing ourselves that gives us strength."
~ Julia Cameron

METHOD THREE

My Beliefs About Love & Relationships

"Nothing binds you except your thoughts; nothing limits you except your fear; and nothing controls you except your beliefs."

~Marianne Williamson

e create our belief systems to make sense of the world. Many of these beliefs are unconscious, yet our lives are a manifestation and a mirror reflection of them.

Relationship patterns represent the unconscious beliefs we hold about relationships. Unconsciously, we think that our beliefs are real and true; therefore, we will search for evidence in our lives to prove their veracity.

It's important to understand that our lives – including our love relationships – move in the direction of our predominant thoughts and beliefs, whether these are "good" and healthy beliefs, or negative and disempowering ones.

Answer the following questions to understand your underlying beliefs about men, love and relationships.

1. I believe relationships are _____

_____

_____

_____

_____

2. I believe men are _____

_____

_____

_____

_____

3. I believe women are _____

_____

_____

_____

_____

4. Sex is _____

_____

_____

_____

_____

5. In a relationship, I believe I deserve _____

_____

_____

_____

_____

_____

_____

_____

6. I believe marriage is _____

_____

_____

_____

_____

_____

_____

_____

_____

"The more you see yourself as what you'd like to become, and act as if what you want is already there, the more you'll activate those dormant forces that will collaborate to transform your dream into your reality."

~Wayne Dyer

7. Describe your childhood and current relationship with your father _____

_____

_____

_____

_____

_____

8. What I learned about men/women and relationships from my father is

_____

_____

_____

_____

_____

_____

_____

9. The partners I attract for relationships resemble my father by

_____

_____

_____

_____

_____

_____

10. Describe your childhood and current relationship with your mother _____

_____

_____

_____

_____

_____

_____

11. What I learned about men/women and relationships from my mother is _____

_____

_____

_____

_____

_____

_____

_____

12. The partners I attract for relationships resemble my mother by _____

_____

_____

_____

_____

_____

13. I believe finding love is _____

_____

_____

_____

_____

_____

14. My role models in relationships are _____

_____

_____

_____

_____

15. I learned from them that relationships are _____

_____

_____

_____

_____

_____

_____

_____

_____

_____

_____

_____

_____

16. What are the new beliefs you would like to hold about love and relationships?

_____

_____

_____

_____

_____

_____

_____

_____

_____

17. Dating today is _____

_____

_____

_____

_____

_____

_____

_____

_____

_____

What did you learn about yourself from this section?

_____

_____

_____

_____

_____

_____

_____

_____

_____

_____

_____

_____

_____

_____

_____

_____

_____

_____

_____

_____

_____

_____

_____

_____

What did you learn about yourself from your date?

_____

_____

_____

_____

_____

_____

_____

_____

_____

_____

_____

_____

_____

_____

_____

_____

_____

_____

_____

_____

_____

_____

_____

_____

_____

Affirmations:

I deeply and completely love and accept myself.

I am in a loving and committed relationship with a faithful, loving, and loyal partner.

I deserve love. I deserve to give and receive love.

Loving relationships and experiences flow to me easily and naturally.

I am a magnet for love.

I am deserving and worthy of a loving relationship.

Write your own affirmations here:

_____

_____

_____

_____

_____

_____

_____

_____

"Faith is expectancy. You do not receive what you want; you do not receive what you pray for, not even what you say you have faith in. You will always receive what you actually expect."
~Eric Butterworth

METHOD FOUR

Understanding My Core Values & Ideal Partner

"Define your priorities, know your values and believe in your purpose. Only then can you effectively share yourself with others."

~Les Brown

When magnetizing a relationship toward us, it's imperative that we know what we desire in a partner. What are our core values? What values are important for our partners to possess?

Without knowing our own needs and desires in a relationship, specifically around how we need to be loved by our partners, or which qualities and characteristics in a partner are important to us, we won't know what to search for or how to recognize our ideal relationship when it shows up. Moreover, we could find ourselves settling for toxic people or those who are simply not our ideal match.

When we buy a new house or a new car or search for a new job, we take strategic action. We make a list of pros and cons. We seek understanding of our needs and desires so that we can create the best match. We consider investment, functionality, practicality, location, etc. Why should we put any less effort into dating? Choosing a partner is an enormous decision; in fact, it can completely alter the trajectory of our lives. So it's important that we give considerable thought, awareness, and attention to making this powerful choice.

We need to be intentional in our approach and do the necessary groundwork. We need to be able to answer the questions: *Who am I? What do I want?*

This section will help you crystallize the vision for your ideal mate as well as help you to better understand yourself and your goals in partnership.

Journal answers to the following questions to gain greater clarity of yourself and your ideal mate.

1. My relationship goals are _____

_____

_____

_____

_____

_____

_____

2. I would like to be in a relationship because _____

_____

_____

_____

_____

_____

3. My 10 most important core values are _____

_____

_____

_____

_____

_____

_____

4. The values I'd like in my partner are _____

_____

_____

_____

_____

_____

_____

5. List your "non-negotiables" and "deal-breakers" in a relation-ship:

a._____

b._____

c._____

d._____

e._____

f._____

g._____

6. The purpose of a relationship is _____

_____

_____

_____

_____

_____

_____

7. Five marriages I admire are:

a. _____

b. _____

c. _____

d. _____

e. _____

"When your values are clear to you, making decisions becomes easier."

~Roy E. Disney

8. My ideal partner is _____

_____

_____

_____

_____

_____

_____

_____

_____

_____

_____

9. My ideal partner looks like _____

_____

_____

_____

_____

_____

_____

_____

_____

10. It's important that my partner _____

_____

_____

_____

_____

_____

_____

_____

_____

_____

_____

11. List your 10 most essential "needs" from a relationship:

a. _____

b. _____

c. _____

d. _____

e. _____

f. _____

g. _____

h. _____

i. _____

j. _____

12. List your 10 "wants" in a partner (the bonuses):

a. _____

b. _____

c. _____

d. _____

e. _____

f. _____

g. _____

h. _____

i. _____

j. _____

12. I feel loved when my partner _____

_____

_____

_____

_____

_____

_____

_____

13. It angers me when my partner _____

_____

_____

_____

_____

_____

_____

_____

14. I couldn't live without _____ in a relationship

_____

_____

_____

_____

15. My goal for dating is _____

_____

_____

_____

_____

_____

_____

_____

_____

_____

_____

16. I believe marriage is _____

_____

_____

_____

_____

_____

_____

_____

_____

_____

_____

What did you learn about your core values after review-ing your entries?

_____

_____

_____

_____

_____

_____

_____

_____

_____

_____

_____

_____

_____

_____

_____

_____

_____

_____

_____

_____

_____

_____

What did you learn about yourself from your date?

Affirmations:

I deeply and completely love and accept myself just as I am.

I attract a relationship that reflects my core values.

I have a loving and compatible relationship with my ideal partner.

Write your own affirmations here:

_____

_____

_____

_____

_____

_____

_____

_____

"Happiness is that state of consciousness which proceeds from the achievement of one's values."
~Ayn Rand

METHOD FIVE

Fear & Sabotage in Relationships

"If we deny love that is given to us, if we refuse to give love because we fear pain or loss, then our lives will be empty, our loss greater."

~Unknown

*U*nderstanding our fears and forms of self-sabotage are important if we want to build and maintain a lasting partnership.

If our fear is greater than what we desire, then our fears will keep our desires at bay.

If we don't recognize our fears when they show up, we may automatically fall into old patterns of behavior that may either keep a relationship away or end one before it has a chance to blossom.

In relationships, fear can look like: fear of commitment; fear of betrayal; fear of abandonment or rejection; fear of success; fear of actually getting what we want; fear of loss; fear of death of our partners; fear that we are unworthy; fear of losing oneself; fear of changing; fear of separation; fear of loneliness; fear of judgment; fear of vulnerability; fear of divorce; fear of intimacy; fear of failure; fear of being "found out"; fear of not being good enough; and so on and so on.

It's no wonder that many relationships fail, because out of the gate we are showing up with conscious and unconscious fears.

Our fears can often be found in the negative relationship patterns that continually show up, such as, "If I keep choosing someone long distance or someone emotionally unavailable, I won't have to commit. I won't have to expose myself and be vulnerable. I am safe." Vulnerability can be frightening, but we cannot experience true love and intimacy without it.

Fear may impede our pursuit of a relationship or keep us stuck in the wrong relationship. Fear can cause us to sabotage the relationship that we say we want.

Journal answers to the following questions to examine how fear may be showing up in your relationships.

1. I am most afraid of _____

_____

_____

_____

_____

2. In a relationship I am frightened the most by _____

_____

_____

_____

_____

3. I learned this fear from _____

_____

_____

_____

_____

4. My fear sounds like _____

_____

_____

_____

_____

5. Vulnerability makes me feel _____

_____

_____

_____

_____

6. I struggle with vulnerability and transparency because ____

_____

_____

_____

_____

7. Fear is keeping me from _____

_____

_____

_____

_____

"Fear is the great enemy of intimacy. Fear makes us run away from each other or cling to each other but does not create true intimacy."

~Henri Nouwen

8. If I didn't have any fear I would _____

_____

_____

_____

_____

_____

_____

9. Commitment makes me feel _____

_____

_____

_____

_____

_____

_____

10. The worst thing that can happen is _____

_____

_____

_____

_____

_____

THE SECRET METHOD TO CONSCIOUS LOVE

11. When I'm afraid I _____

_____

_____

_____

_____

_____

_____

12. I blame my partner when _____

_____

_____

_____

_____

_____

_____

13. Fear keeps me from _____

_____

_____

_____

_____

_____

_____

14. I am afraid to be judged for _____

_____

_____

_____

_____

_____

_____

_____

_____

_____

_____

15. In a relationship I feel angry when _____

_____

_____

_____

_____

_____

_____

_____

_____

_____

What did you learn about yourself from this section?

_____

_____

_____

_____

_____

_____

_____

_____

_____

_____

_____

_____

_____

_____

_____

_____

_____

_____

_____

_____

_____

_____

_____

What did you learn about yourself from your date?

_____

_____

_____

_____

_____

_____

_____

_____

_____

_____

_____

_____

_____

_____

_____

_____

_____

_____

_____

_____

_____

_____

_____

_____

Affirmations:

I deeply and completely love and approve of myself.

It is okay for me to be afraid but I still choose love.

It is safe for me to be vulnerable.

I overcome my challenges with grace and ease.

It is safe for me to speak my truth to others.

Write your own affirmations here:

_____

_____

_____

_____

_____

_____

_____

"Living with fear stops us from taking risks, and if you don't go out on the branch, you're never going to get the best fruit."
~Sarah Parish

METHOD SIX

Letting Go Through Forgiveness

"Forgiveness is not an occasional act; it is a constant attitude."

~Dr. Martin Luther King, Jr.

*I*n order to manifest love, we want our hearts to be as free and unencumbered as possible. However, our hearts cannot fully open to give and receive love in a new relationship if we're still harboring old resentments, wounds and anger.

Forgiveness is the antidote, softening our hearts to allow more love in and to create healthier relationships devoid of the "ghosts" of partners past. Forgiveness is a journey — a lifetime process. Like peeling back the layers of an onion, we peel back one layer to see that we have more layers to remove. Embrace where you are in your forgiveness journey. Try not to judge or condemn yourself. Forgiveness is not condoning your perpetrators behavior, nor is it granting them renewed trust. Forgiveness is reclaiming pieces of your heart and power. It is an act of self love. We will also look at where we might need to be forgiven by others — to take accountability for our own actions.

Journal answers to the following questions to explore your relationship and call for forgiveness.

1. Forgiveness means _____

_____

_____

_____

2. It's hard for me to forgive because _____

_____

_____

_____

3. I need to forgive _____ for _____

_____

_____

_____

4. I need to forgive _____ for _____

_____

_____

_____

5. I need to forgive _____ for _____

_____

_____

6. I need to forgive _____ for _____

_____

_____

_____

7. I need to forgive _____ for _____

_____

_____

8. I am angry at _____ for _____

_____

_____

_____

9. I am angry at _____ for _____

_____

_____

_____

"I think the first step is to understand that forgiveness does not exonerate the perpetrator. Forgiveness liberates the victim. It's a gift you give yourself."

~ T.D. Jakes

10. I need to forgive myself for _____

_____

_____

_____

11. I need to forgive myself for _____

_____

_____

_____

12. I need to forgive myself for _____

_____

_____

_____

13. I need to forgive myself for _____

_____

_____

_____

14. I need to forgive myself for _____

_____

_____

_____

15. I forgive my father for _____

_____

_____

_____

16. I forgive my mother for _____

_____

_____

_____

_____

17. I am sorry for _____

_____

_____

_____

"Forgiveness is giving up the hope that the past could have been any different."

~Oprah Winfrey

18. I can't forgive _____ for _____

_____

_____

_____

19. List all of the things you are willing to release:

a. _____

b. _____

c. _____

d. _____

e. _____

f. _____

g. _____

h. _____

i. _____

j. _____

20. I take responsibility for _____

_____

_____

_____

_____

_____

21. The potential "ghosts" between me and my partner are __

_____

_____

_____

_____

_____

A BUDDHIST PRAYER OF FORGIVENESS

If I have harmed anyone in any way,

either knowingly or unknowingly

through my own confusions,

I ask their forgiveness.

If anyone has harmed me in any way,

either knowingly or unknowingly

through their own confusions,

I forgive them.

And if there is a situation

I am not yet ready to forgive,

I forgive myself for that.

For all the ways that I harm myself, negate, doubt,

belittle myself, judge or be unkind to myself, through

my own confusions,

I forgive myself.

What did you learn about yourself from this section?

_____

_____

_____

_____

_____

_____

_____

_____

_____

_____

_____

_____

_____

_____

_____

_____

_____

_____

_____

_____

_____

What did you learn about yourself from your date?

_____

_____

_____

_____

_____

_____

_____

_____

_____

_____

_____

_____

_____

_____

_____

_____

_____

_____

_____

_____

_____

_____

Affirmations:

I deeply and completely love and accept myself.

I forgive myself and others for any harm they've caused me.

I forgive _____ for _____.

I did the best I could with the information and awareness I had at the time.

I choose loving thoughts about myself.

I forgive myself for every hurtful word and action I have ever committed against myself.

I am patient with myself to forgive.

Write your own affirmations here:

_____

_____

_____

_____

_____

_____

_____

"If we really want to love we must learn how to forgive."
~Mother Theresa

METHOD SEVEN

Recognizing My Emotional Wounds & Triggers

"If you are irritated by every rub, how will your mirror be polished?"

~Rumi

Relationships serve as our teachers, oftentimes by unearthing old wounds and giving us opportunities to clear them. Romantic partnerships in particular will trigger us, so it's important that we know and understand our wounds and their root causes so that we can properly address them with our partners, respond more effectively, and work toward healing them.

It's not fun when someone pokes at an old scab and wound. The wounded child in us wants to lash out and protect ourselves. We may respond angrily, project our wounds onto our partners, or displace anger from our original source of pain onto them. However, if we understand our triggers, are able to comfort ourselves with forgiveness and compassion, and can articulate how we are feeling in an authentic way, we will be able to heal them.

Write answers to the following questions to discover and understand your relationship emotional triggers.

1. It hurts me most when _____

_____

_____

_____

_____

2. It hurts me when my partner _____

_____

_____

_____

_____

3. I am most afraid in a relationship of _____

_____

_____

_____

_____

4. It frightens me when _____

_____

_____

_____

_____

5. I am happiest when _____

_____

_____

_____

_____

6. I feel abandoned when _____

_____

_____

_____

_____

7. I feel betrayed when _____

_____

_____

_____

_____

"Once you uncover the history of this pattern and trace its roots, you will see that your reaction in the present moment is really a reaction from the past, a shadow character's attempt to protect you from re-experiencing an old emotional wound, which instead sabotages you in the present."

~Connie Zweig

8. Things that bring me joy are _____

_____

_____

_____

_____

9. I am angriest when my partner _____

_____

_____

_____

_____

10. I am saddest when _____

_____

_____

_____

_____

11. I feel alone when _____

_____

_____

_____

_____

12. When I am alone I _____

_____

_____

_____

_____

13. I feel loved when _____

_____

_____

_____

_____

14. List your emotional triggers here that have shown up in past relationships:

a. _____

b. _____

c. _____

d. _____

e. _____

f. _____

g. _____

h. _____

i. _____

j. _____

What did you learn about yourself from this section?

_____

_____

_____

_____

_____

_____

_____

_____

_____

_____

_____

_____

_____

_____

_____

_____

_____

_____

_____

_____

_____

_____

What did you learn about yourself from your date?

Affirmations:

I deeply and completely love and approve of myself.

I am always safe and protected.

I embrace my inner child and her needs.

It is safe for me to be in a loving relationship.

Write your own affirmations here:

_____

_____

_____

_____

_____

_____

_____

"The real challenge is to remember to see clearly when everything's flying around us and we're wrapped up in our [emotional] wounds and traumas."

~Mark Nepo

METHOD EIGHT

Building Confidence

"There is nothing more rare, nor more beautiful, than a woman being unapologetically herself; comfortable in her perfect imperfection. To me, that is the true essence of beauty."

~Steve Maraboli

*I*n this last section, we address confidence. I consider confidence one of the most important attributes that each partner can possess in a healthy and loving relationship. When one is lacking in confidence and self-esteem, even if only for a brief period, it has the potential to deteriorate the relationship.

As mentioned earlier in this workbook, our personal happiness is not the responsibility of another. That goes for our confidence as well. Building and maintaining confidence is an inside job. No one else can make us "feel" more confident.

For example, if we don't feel good about our looks or some other aspect of ourselves, there is no amount of flirting and complimenting our partner can do to make up for it. Any wonderful message they deliver will sound disingenuous, because we don't believe it about ourself.

Relationships thrive best when both parties are confident with themselves and bring two separate, whole, and complete beings together. Confidence is a learned behavior. Some of us develop it at an early age and maintain it throughout adulthood. Others learn it later in life and need to practice it until it becomes second nature.

While dating, confidence is going to be essential to attracting partners to us. Potential relationship suitors love confidence. They can sniff it miles away. The same is true for desperation and insecurity.

That said, confidence is ultimately very attractive to both men and women. Why? Because when we are genuinely confident (this is not to be confused with egotism and grandiosity), we are making a stake in our self-worth. When we are confident we feel good about ourselves and confident in what we deserve. For instance, a man desires to be with a woman who believes she deserves someone great, because it mirrors back to him that he is good and worthy. What does it say to a man that chooses a woman who doesn't feel great about herself?

Confidence speaks before we do. It enters the room first and has the power to own it. When we show up confident in a relationship we let our partners know that we are not seeking approval, which can be a heavy and taxing burden on any relationship. Instead, we show up already filled up and approving of ourselves. We aren't looking for any voids or emptiness to be filled by our partner. We have filled them already.

Giving God-sized needs to another human being
will constantly disappoint us.

Journal answers to the following questions about confidence.

1. I feel most confident when _____

_____

_____

_____

_____

2. I feel least confident when _____

_____

_____

_____

_____

3. My strengths are _____

_____

_____

_____

_____

4. My weaknesses are _____

_____

_____

_____

_____

5. My past successes in career, relationships, family, sports/ awards, education, are _____

_____

_____

_____

_____

6. Five new goals that I want to accomplish in the future are:

a._____

b._____

c._____

d._____

e._____

7. From my past "mistakes" and "failures" I learned _____

_____

_____

_____

_____

8. When I help others I feel _____ I can help others by

_____

_____

_____

_____

_____

9. When I look in the mirror I feel _____

_____

_____

_____

_____

10. Ten nice things I can say about myself include:

a._____

b._____

c._____

d._____

e._____

f._____

g._____

h._____

i._____

j._____

11. Which activities or risks can I take outside of my comfort zone that will bolster my confidence? _____

_____

_____

_____

_____

_____

What did you learn about yourself from this section?

_____

_____

_____

_____

_____

_____

_____

_____

_____

_____

_____

_____

_____

_____

_____

_____

_____

_____

_____

_____

_____

_____

What did learn about yourself from your date?

_____

_____

_____

_____

_____

_____

_____

_____

_____

_____

_____

_____

_____

_____

_____

_____

_____

_____

_____

_____

_____

_____

Affirmations

I deeply and completely love and approve of myself.

I am strong, beautiful, whole, and complete.

Confidence comes easily and naturally to me.

I am confident in my strengths and I embrace my weaknesses.

I choose to be confident.

Write your own affirmations here:

_____

_____

_____

_____

_____

_____

_____

"Every woman that finally figured out her worth, has picked up her suitcases of pride and boarded a flight to freedom, which landed in the valley of change."
~Shannon L. Alder

EPILOGUE

"Love recognizes no barriers. It jumps hurdles, leaps fences, penetrates walls to arrive at its destination full of hope."

~Maya Angelou

In reaching the end of this journal and completing all of the exercises, you ought to have discovered a deeper understanding of yourself and greater awareness of your patterns and behaviors in relationships. Self-awareness is the first critical step in creating change in our lives.

Now, with your greater awareness, the next steps are to notice which of your behavioral practices and patterns are no longer serving you in a relationship. What keeps getting in your way of creating a long-term, healthy relationship? Which of your behaviors do you wish to change? Where do you notice additional healing is needed in order to move forward and open up to love that honors you? Which relationship skills could you further practice?

It's never too late to change and grow. It requires a decision, commitment, and practice. And if you'd like to expand further in your relationship growth and attract healthier relationships, my 8-week online course:

The Conscious Love & Dating Method™: Become The ONE You Want & Attract The Love You Desire, is a powerful next step to support you in attracting and sustaining love. Women who complete the course are changing their own dating narrative, learning and practicing powerful tools for partnership, breaking old relationship patterns, and healing old wounds. They're having more dates and more fun, sometimes after years without dating.

Here are a few words by women that have completed the course:

"Angela and her Conscious Love & Dating Method Course came at just right time and saved my life after a painful and challenging break-up. Breakups can take a toll on your life, but having Angela in my corner, coaching me, praying for me, guiding me...I have to pinch myself because I'm doing so well. Angela gives, gives, gives. From affirmations, prayers, self love practices, meditations, readings, the list goes on and on. And she's always there to give advice and get you through tough times. It's often hard to admit that we don't love ourselves enough, Angela let me know that it was okay and taught me how to love myself. She helped me through tough moments with inspiring talk, scripture and a few words of wisdom. Since then, I'm truly loving myself more and more and looking forward to meeting my soulmate. I never wanted the course to end. I am so grateful for Angela & all of her work and guidance, I could not have gone through this time without her. Angela is a blessing, whose passion is changing the lives of the women she touches."

~ Jana S., Detroit, Michigan

"Angela is an incredible teacher! The course was in a group setting, and even still, Angela had a wonderful way of catering to each person in a compassionate, friendly, personal, non-judgmental way. Highly recommended for anyone looking to improve their love life, inner life, professional life - it's all encompassing. Feeling lighter, more optimistic and excited about my journey ahead. Thank you, Angela, for your wisdom and insight!!"

~ Janet C., Long Island, NY

"This course was the most rewarding undertaking I have ever done. You were felt, validated and important each and every week. The course got all of us to be close friends that were willing to share our private feelings and joys and sorrows. It was just a wonderful event. Angela is a gem and she is worth her weight in gold. I would do more courses with her...thank you for such a wonderful course. [Angela] is such a kind person and so easy to open up too. She has a true gift. Spirit has blessed [her] with a Mother Teresa gift of helping people."

~ Judy B., PA

** (Judy, a beautiful woman in her 60's is now engaged and set to be married in May 2021 to a wonderful man she met while enrolled in the course during the pandemic.) **

"Angela and her Conscious Love & Dating Method Course have helped me in ways that have truly changed the course of my life. The Course helped me dig deep and look at myself through a different lens; one that I've needed to see through for a very long time. I realized that I had been dating ALL wrong. It wasn't about them; it was about ME! Angela has shown me how to truly love myself and for the first time ever in my life, I fell in love with MYSELF during her course. I realized that I don't need anyone to complete me. I am complete and whole all on my own. That, to me, is priceless. I am now ready and better equipped to welcome in a beautiful partnership into my life."

~ Karina M., New York City

"I enrolled in Angela's course a single person who was 100% anti-online dating, and ended the course in a new relationship with a wonderful man who I met online! We have now been together for over two years. I would not have opened up to online dating if it wasn't for Angela's insight, perspective and advice. Angela is invested in her students. She took time to speak to each of us directly about where we were in the process and in our lives. I am all around in a better place since taking Angela's Conscious Love & Dating Method Course and have grown as a person. I still use my tools, especially as my new relationship continues to blossom."

~ Porsche, New York City

"Angela's course was amazing. It reminded me to focus on my own growth and development while seeking love and romantic partnership. I loved all of the tools and resources Angela provided for us. I know I will go back to those resources for months, if not years, to come. I also appreciated the community of women who were vulnerable and open with one another, and shared their growth journey through this process. This was definitely money well spent because it was the best investment I could make --back into myself. I highly recommend this course!"

~ Ola F., New York City

Angela truly is and has been a monumental gift in my life. She carries a pure Mother Teresa light that shines and blesses everyone who comes into contact with her. I feel so fortunate to have been blessed by her magical touch and loving guidance....I had resisted online dating for so long, and honestly I have to share that it s been a game changer, not just because of taking this action, more importantly because of the conscious intention behind everything Angela does, holds space for and teaches. As soon as you enter this course, you will feel the miraculous touch of love and transformation immediately...I felt God s presence with us our entire journey, and I made life long sisterhood for life, this is priceless. My concept of love has undergone a deep renewal and rebirth. I am more prepared for love than I have ever been. Angela s course is life changing, and please note, this course is NOT just for someone who wants to date or find love, it s absolutely for you, if you have lost touch with yourself...I am so grateful for Angela and so glad I said yes, because it is not only shifting my personal life, my professional life is blooming, my confidence has sky-rocketed, and I am forever humbled by the power of conscious, intentional love."

~ Astraya, California

"Angela's guidance brought me not only closer to my femininity but in my relationship with God. I gained more in the two months working with Angela in the course then in 4 years of therapy."

~ Ayanna, Maryland

To learn more about the course visit:
www.lovesanctuary.com

To contact Angela write to: info@lovesanctuary.com

Freestyle Journaling

(Feel free to doodle, draw, and express your feelings creatively)

Journaling Notes

_____

_____

_____

_____

_____

_____

_____

_____

_____

_____

_____

_____

_____

_____

_____

_____

_____

_____

ABOUT THE AUTHOR

*A*ngela became a Dating and Relationship Coach and created The Conscious Love & Dating Method™ because she saw the extreme need to change the current dating landscape.

She wants to share the transformational tools she has gathered along her own dating and educational journey with women who are confused and overwhelmed in today's dating culture.

Her mission is to revolutionize dating and relationships and inspire women to create dating relationships with greater intention, self-awareness, and self-love.

Angela currently lives in Colorado but feels most at home when she's near the ocean.

ACKNOWLEDGMENTS

*T*hank you to my Supreme Power who has entrusted me with this assignment. I humbly serve you.

Love and gratitude to you Mom & Daddy, your unconditional love fuels me. To my grandmothers who are still rocking it out in their 90's - you inspire me daily. My Dearest Aunt Carol, my sisters, and my only brother — thank you, with love! Thank you to my multitude of cousins and dear friends. To my Divine team, thank you for answering the *call!* And thank you to my furry angel in heaven, you continue to guide me.

Made in United States
North Haven, CT
02 July 2022

20896588R00070